Our suffering Savior

―――∞∞∞―――

DAILY DEVOTIONS

Copyright © 2006 Concordia Publishing House
3558 S. Jefferson Ave., St. Louis, MO 63118-3968
1-800-325-3040 • www.cph.org

All rights reserved. Unless specifically noted, no part of this publication may be reproduced, stored in a retrieval system, or transmitted, in any form or by any means, electronic, mechanical, photocopying, recording, or otherwise, without the prior written permission of Concordia Publishing House.

Scripture quotations are from The Holy Bible, English Standard Version, copyright © 2001 by Crossway Bibles, a division of Good News Publishers. Used by permission. All rights reserved.

Hymn texts with the abbreviation *LW* are from *Lutheran Worship*, copyright © 1982 Concordia Publishing House. All rights reserved.

Hymn texts with the abbreviation *TLH* are from *The Lutheran Hymnal*, copyright © 1941 Concordia Publishing House. All rights reserved.

Hymn texts with the abbreviation *HS98* are from *Hymnal Supplement 98*, copyright © 1998 Concordia Publishing House. All rights reserved.

The abbreviation *LSB* refers to *Lutheran Service Book*, copyright © 2006 Concordia Publishing House. All rights reserved.

Quotes from *Luther's Small Catechism with Explanation*, copyright © 1986, 1991 Concordia Publishing House. All rights reserved.

Manufactured in the United States of America

Library of Congress Cataloging-in-Publication Data

Snyder, Walter.
Our Suffering Savior daily devotions / Walter Snyder.
  p. cm
ISBN 0-7586-1025-4
1. Bible. O.T. Isaiah LIII—Mediations. 2. Servent of Jehovah—Mediations. 3. Jesus Christ—Serventhood—Meditations. 4. Bible. O.T. Isaiah—Meditations. 5. Church year meditations. I. Title. BS1515.6.S4S69 2006
242'.34—dc22
                          2006014497

1 2 3 4 5 6 7 8 9 10   15 14 13 12 11 10 09 08 07 06

Our suffering Savior

DAILY DEVOTIONS

WALTER SNYDER

CONCORDIA PUBLISHING HOUSE · SAINT LOUIS

Ash Wednesday
& the Days Following

ASH WEDNESDAY

READ ISAIAH 52:13–53:12
PSALM 106:1–12

Can You Believe It!

The exclamation point in the heading is intentional. The prophet Isaiah does more than ask if we trust this summation of the work of the Suffering Servant. He presents the events in such manner as to shake the mind and stir the soul.

An early American hymn declares: "What wondrous love is this, O my soul, O my soul!" Sometimes we forget that Lent, every bit as much as the Christmas season or Eastertide, is a time of *wonder*.

The wonder of God's grace embodied in the Suffering Servant challenges our minds just as much as do the marvels of the incarnation and resurrection. The Old Adam resists repenting of its evil while our sin-diminished comprehension, in Thomas-like disbelief, challenges God to make certain the truth.

The Small Catechism's explanation of the Third Article of the Creed says, "I believe that I cannot by my own reason or strength believe . . ." (p. 15). Yet the Holy Spirit, working through God's living and active Word, creates and sustains faith. As our Lenten pilgrimage walks us through all that our Savior did and continues to do for us, we can rest assured that God will use His Son's Passion to continue convicting us of our sins, to forgive us of all unrighteousness, and to grow and sustain confidence in our salvation through Him who died for us:

What wondrous love is this, O my soul, O my soul!
What wondrous love is this, O my soul!
What wondrous love is this That caused the Lord of bliss
To bear the dreadful curse for my soul, for my soul,
To bear the dreadful curse for my soul! (*HS98* 860:1 [*LSB* 543])

Lord God, grant that we receive with faith and wonder the benefits of Your Son's sacrificial service on our behalf. Amen.

THURSDAY AFTER ASH WEDNESDAY

READ MATTHEW 3:13–17
PSALM 2

Another Fine Mess

In Jesus' Baptism, the Father announced that He was installing the Son into the office of Suffering Servant. The first Servant Song begins, "Behold my servant, whom I uphold, my chosen, in whom my soul delights; I have put my Spirit upon him; he will bring forth justice to the nations" (Isaiah 42:1).

Notice the intentional parallel from the Lord's Baptism: The Father delighted in the Son and visibly placed the Holy Spirit upon Him. He also placed Jesus squarely in the midst of the mess of sinful mankind. Jesus voluntarily assumed our humanity, becoming a man that He might rescue man from the infernal "mess" of sin, death, and eternal damnation.

Christ's Baptism connected the Person with the prophecies. Here, in the Jordan River, stood the "Head crusher" of Genesis 3:15. The One in whom the Father delighted took upon Himself the responsibility and the guilt for all mankind's messes—not one of which is truly "fine." Even as the Father delighted in Him, He also drove the Son into the Wilderness, where Jesus would begin an ongoing time of testing and temptation.

Delighting in Christ's obedient service, the Father heaped on Him the crushing weight of all our sins of thought, word, and deed. God's Son, who knew no sin, became sin—our sin—as John washed Him with the water of our repentance.

Thank You, Lord Jesus, for taking our sins upon Yourself and for paying the price for our unbelief. Amen.

FRIDAY AFTER ASH WEDNESDAY

READ EPHESIANS 2:8–10
PSALM 15

Who Has Done?

Isaiah asked, "Who has believed?" We do well, also, to ask, "Who has done?" Who has done the will of the Lord? Who always obeyed and never strayed? Who kept the Law perfectly in thought, word, and deed? Who loved the Lord His God with total commitment of heart, mind, and soul? Who always loved His neighbor as Himself?

Of course, you're saying, "Jesus!" Yet in faith, you *may* say, "I did!" The Servant's suffering allows us to receive His righteousness as our reward. Saved by grace through faith in Christ, God sets us in a life of good works. Even more, He calls us to wear Christ's works, counting us righteous not for what we've done but for what Jesus did.

We cannot trust our own works; all our righteousness is a polluted garment fit for hell's eternal burn pile (Isaiah 64:6). We *must*, however, trust in the work of the Suffering Servant. Because He always spoke truly, the Father counts our speech as clean. Because He always acted in love, the Father considers us to be models of compassion. Because He always attended to His Father's will, the Father names us as "good and faithful servants" (Matthew 25:21).

We passively receive credit for the Servant's actions. The forgiveness and righteousness we could not achieve for ourselves become ours on account of the Father's Suffering Servant. These same gifts move us to action. We seek out our Father's Word and will and commit ourselves to pouring out His love upon neighbor and enemy alike. Scarcely able to believe our own good fortune, He guides us to share His wealth with the unfortunate struggling under sin's oppression.

Jesus, Your blood and righteousness
My beauty are, my glorious dress;
Mid flaming worlds, in these arrayed,
With joy shall I lift up my head. Amen. (LW 362:1 [LSB 563])

Daily Devotions

Even the Demons Believe

Who believed the word about the Suffering Servant? Satan surely did. After Jesus' Baptism, the devil took full advantage of the forty days of wilderness fasting to test the Son's resolve. If the anointing of the Messiah in Jordan's baptismal waters was God's declaration of war, Satan showed himself immediately ready to counterattack.

The devil took God's Word more seriously than we often do. In response to Christ's threat against his power, Satan engaged in all-out battle, continuing the war he'd begun with his initial rebellion. Even before Jesus' Baptism signaled God's escalation of hostilities against demonic power, the devil showed that he believed the threat of Genesis 3: "He shall bruise your head." His diabolical scheming led to Herod's fears and the slaughter of Bethlehem's little boys (Matthew 2:16–18).

We don't want "faith" like the devil's. James reminds us that Satan "shudders" in fear at what he knows. However, this same knowledge causes Christians to "shiver with delight." The demons dread the might of the One who bore their hatred even as He endured the Father's wrath at our sins. They know that Christ broke their reign of darkness forever during the dark hours on the cross. Satan invested all his might trying to destroy Christ, lying to Christ, to Herod, to the Jewish leaders, and to Pilate.

All of these lies went for naught. Christ trusted in His Father's plan of salvation. He carried it out to perfection. He grants salvation to all who believe in Him, to all who know Him not as dread enemy but closest comfort.

> *Bruise for me the Serpent's head*
> *That, set free from doubt and dread,*
> *I may cling to You in faith,*
> *Safely kept through life and death. Amen.* (*LW* 33:6 [*LSB* 352])

Lent
Week One

FIRST SUNDAY IN LENT

READ MARK 9:14–29
PSALM 147:7–11

I Believe . . . But

Who believed? A father did. Day by day, he witnessed his dear son's suffering. He saw the agony inflicted by the demon. Powerless, he watched the physical oppression and spiritual torment undergone by his child.

In contrast, we see how the Suffering Servant completely took our fallen flesh upon Himself. His Father watched Him suffer through Israel's doubt and resistance. The sinless Son of God endured undeserved demonic torment and physical pain in order to remove them from sinful, deserving mankind.

Unable to do anything to aid his beloved son, this father turned to the Son of his heavenly Father. In the midst of tumult generated by a "faithless generation," he asked Jesus of Nazareth, "If you can do anything, have compassion on us and help us."

"If!" We might wonder what tone of voice Jesus used in responding to half-hearted belief. The Lord answers those who trust wholly in Him. He demands a faith we're incapable of developing.

The boy's father realized this, confessing both unworthiness and total dependence upon God's grace: "I believe; help my unbelief!" Counter to human reason, against sinful flesh's doubts, the Holy Spirit moved the man to join the ranks of the faithful even before receiving earthly proof that his prayer would be answered.

Likewise, the Spirit works among us. Questioning, doubting, unbelieving sinners receive answers, assurances, and confidence from their loving God. These character traits of the Suffering Servant become part of our new nature in Him, so that we may pray as the Catechism teaches us, "as dear children ask their dear father" (p. 17).

Dearest Father, grant us the Holy Spirit that we might believe Your promises and trust in Your plan for our lives; through the merits of Jesus our Savior. Amen.

MONDAY, LENT 1 — READ MARK 6:1–6 — PSALM 96

Home Is Where the Unbelief Is

Isaiah foretold the astonishment that would greet the Suffering Servant and His work. Today's reading reminds us that being astonished isn't the same as believing in the One who astonishes.

Jesus returned to His hometown to proclaim the Good News. He longed to remove sin's sickness from those among whom He'd spent His youth. When He began teaching, the congregation was astonished—for the wrong reasons. They weren't bowled over by Jesus' display of God's amazing grace. Instead, they wondered how this fellow they'd known for years could be spouting off the way He did.

Familiarity doesn't always breed con*tempt*. Sometimes, it breeds con*tentment*. Especially if we've grown up in the faith, we think we know it all. We become comfortable with the Jesus we think we know, tuning out His challenges to continuing faithfulness and increasing service. We think of Him more as "one of us" than we do of ourselves as "one of His." Such a faith is as lukewarm as that of Laodicea (Revelation 3:16), where the Lord threatened to spit out such an unpalatable assembly.

Let us pray that Christ would daily renew and revitalize our faith so that He won't marvel at our unbelief and callous reception of His gifts, and that we might receive spiritual healing and life eternal. Let us ask not for casual familiarity but for the ever-exciting intimacy of His indwelling, so we might thrill at His every word:

> *Amazing grace! How sweet the sound*
> *That saved a wretch like me!*
> *I once was lost but now am found,*
> *Was blind but now I see!* (LW 509:1 [LSB 744])

**Lord, we ask that every day and in every way
You would amaze us at the depth of Your sacrifice and
the lavishness of Your love. Amen.**

TUESDAY, LENT 1

READ ACTS 17:10–15
PSALM 42:8–13

Berean Belief

The Old Testament Scriptures created saving faith in those who heard and believed in the Savior who was to come. God promised that the Suffering Servant would come to redeem His Israel. Now that the long-expected Christ has come, salvation is found only in those who call upon Jesus as Savior.

When Paul, Silas, and Timothy came to Berea, they found people already believing that the Messiah would come. They were ready for the revelation of Jesus Christ because His Spirit had already prepared their hearts.

The Bereans knew where to turn when Paul proclaimed the death and resurrection of Jesus for their salvation. They eagerly compared the apostle's testimony with that of the prophets, "examining the Scriptures daily to see if these things were so" (Acts 17:11). Finding out that the message was true, many came into fullness of faith.

In our day, God continues to challenge us to faithfully accept the message that One came to carry our sicknesses, sorrows, and sins on Himself. He encourages us to eagerly search the Scriptures ourselves, that His Word might convince and remind us that Christ's sacrifice brought our release.

When we wonder if God truly cares, He reminds us that the Suffering Servant suffered for us. We trustingly cast our anxieties on Him, knowing that He cares for us (1 Peter 5:7). When evil circumstances tempt us to doubt, the Scriptures say, "Be certain." Because of the Servant's sacrifice, nothing "in all creation, will be able to separate us from the love of God in Christ Jesus our Lord" (Romans 8:39).

Though earth, Lord, break asunder, You are my Savior true;
No fire or sword or thunder Shall sever me from you;
No danger, thirst, or hunger, No pain or poverty,
No mighty princes' anger Shall ever vanquish me. Amen.
(LW 407:4 [LSB 724])

WEDNESDAY, LENT 1
READ ISAIAH 52:14; 53:2–3
PSALM 22:1–18

Deceitful Appearance

"He got what was coming to him!" These words summarize the opinion of those who arranged and observed the death of the Suffering Servant. By the time of His death, He was so battered and tormented that He was almost unrecognizable, not only as Jesus of Nazareth but even as a man.

Torture and crucifixion marred Jesus' appearance. Yet even before His arrest, much about Him was hidden. Yes, the evil that He took upon Himself led to horrible disfigurement. God, however, also hid Himself in Christ during Jesus' entire time on earth. Even now, our "Hidden God" reveals Himself not on our terms but His own.

"Don't judge a book by its cover," reminds us that outward appearances can hide what is really inside. A quick glance at the Christ on the cross can easily confuse the onlooker. In His day, violent criminals and rebels went to the cross while kings rode magnificent horses and led large armies. On the cross Jesus does not look anything like a king. He is hidden.

We often see those disfigured by life and sin and a fallen world. Their outward appearance may make us wonder what they did wrong to have such a miserable life. But if we rely on faith's eyes instead of human intellect and experience, we see that God has switched everything around. The Just suffers for the unjust, the Righteous dies for the sinner. For our benefit, the things of God are seldom as they seem. Even in Bethlehem's manger, God, hidden in human flesh, was working the "Great Exchange" of our evil and its consequences for His mercy and grace.

We are rich, for He was poor;
Is not this a wonder?
Therefore praise God evermore
Here on earth and yonder. Amen. (*LW* 42:3 [*LSB* 390])

READ LUKE 7:24–33
LUKE 1:46–55

THURSDAY, LENT 1

A Song and Dance Routine

Even John the Baptizer had his doubts, it seems. Sitting in Herod's prison, he sent some of his disciples to make absolutely sure that the One he'd proclaimed was the One whom God had sent. John's followers received confirmation in the comparison of God's Word with Jesus' deeds.

Jesus then used John in order to speak to the perceptions and attitudes of those around Him. They wanted God to dance to their tune, to respond as they saw fit. Jesus criticized them for constructing a god according to their own understanding rather than believing in the God revealed in the Word.

In Isaiah 55:8, the Lord reminds us, "My thoughts are not your thoughts, neither are your ways My ways." His funeral dirge is His holy Law, which condemns our sins and crushes our pride. We can't chase away accountability by plugging our ears; nor can we please Him by shouting out a happy tune. The believer weeps over his continual falling into sin as he hears the somber song of God's Law and its absolute demands.

Yet in the midst of our despair over our sins, God plays a joyful tune. Healing us through Christ's blood-bought forgiveness, He calls us to dance for joy. Our hearts leap within us and our actions follow suit. We aren't exiled to the outer darkness of weeping and gnashing of teeth. We're invited to the marriage feast of the Lamb in His kingdom.

My soul doth magnify the Lord,
My spirit shall in God rejoice;
My low estate He did regard,
Exalting me by gracious choice. (TLH 275:1 [LSB 934])

FRIDAY, LENT 1

READ MATTHEW 20:1–16
PSALM 107:10–16

Equal Pay for Unequal Work

Everyday speech is filled with expressions such as "You get what you pay for," and "There's no such thing as a free lunch." While this thinking isn't new, Jesus directs us to see that where salvation is concerned, appearances are quite deceiving.

We often resent others getting more than we think they deserve. We want evil punished, good rewarded, and hard work paid a fair wage. Willing to help those we deem legitimately "down on their luck," we bristle at the thought of supporting freeloaders who could get out and earn their own living.

In the parable of the laborers, Jesus points out that the gifts of the kingdom are just that—*gifts*. The promise of good is in place before anyone does a lick of work. He calls us by the Gospel to live in His kingdom. He takes away our sins, sets us right with God, and gives eternal life *before* He puts us to work on earth.

Christ directs us to look away from our fellow kingdom-workers' motives. Instead, He invites us to examine His work from conception through crucifixion. Rather than compare ourselves to others, He calls us to accept and appreciate His largesse: "Do you begrudge my generosity?"

In this light, we see that we haven't "borne the burden of the day and the scorching heat." After enduring salvation's brutal labor upon His whip-torn body, He invites us to receive as a *gift* the full wage He *earned* from His Father—even though we came late and never labored as did He.

> Cause us, O Lord, to focus not on our own works,
> nor compare ourselves with others, but rather to receive
> with joy our place in the kingdom and steadfastly labor
> through this life in thanksgiving. Amen.

Daily Devotions

SATURDAY, LENT 1

READ COLOSSIANS 3:1–17
PSALM 45:1–9

Bug-Ugly to Butterfly-Beautiful

The life cycle of the butterfly became an early illustration of the resurrection and of our new life in Christ. The worm-like, often ugly caterpillar entered the "tomb" of the chrysalis, only to come to beautifully winged new life.

Unless one is familiar with these insects, drawing a direct comparison between caterpillar and butterfly appears ridiculous. And who expects anything living, let alone beautiful, to emerge from the lifeless cocoon after it sits all winter in a cold, bleak meadow?

To the world, we may appear as worthless worms. Our worth may not amount to much by secular reckoning. Paul invites the Colossian Christians (and us) to see beyond surface appearance. In Baptism, we've already died by participating in Christ's death. Even as we draw breath on earth, we already anticipate breathing heaven's air in our glorious resurrection bodies.

Sometimes glimpses of the new creature peek out, especially as we trust Christ and go about His Father's business. Mostly, though, only God sees what He has already made us to be—what will be publicly revealed on the Last Day.

As we continue living here, our true lives safely concealed in Christ, we remember that for our sake, He reversed the process. He who was wholly beautiful of His own nature forsook heavenly glory. He became one of us "worms" that He might remake us into butterflies. He became our beautiful Savior by assuming the hideous visage of our sinfulness.

Even before we receive the fullness of our new natures, He enables us through Word and Spirit to cast off the vile trappings of fallen man and to wear the robes of righteousness He imparts.

Beautiful Savior, King of creation,
Son of God and Son of Man!
Truly I'd love Thee, Truly I'd serve Thee,
Light of my soul, my joy, my crown. Amen (LW 507:1 [LSB 537])

Lent

Week Two

SECOND SUNDAY IN LENT

READ GENESIS 50:15–21
PSALM 69:1–15

God's Hidden Good

Some folks say that "if life gives you lemons, make lemonade." But what if life gives you a dysfunctional family, violent assault, kidnapping, lies about your reputation, imprisonment, and abandonment by those you befriend?

Joseph couldn't have constructed a stand large enough to sell all the lemonade from his life's lemons. He couldn't ignore everything that had been done to him. He knew full well the magnitude of the evil his brothers intended. He also knew how God had used him as an instrument of salvation, setting him in place to save Jacob's family when famine struck.

We might hesitate in approaching God because of the magnitude of our own sins. We know that we have sinned and done evil in His sight. We know He abhors wickedness and may be too fearful or ashamed to come into His presence.

Joseph's brothers feared that he'd been treating them well for Jacob's sake. Now that Dad was dead, wouldn't little brother give them what they deserved? No. Joseph recognized the hand of the Lord in his life and rejoiced in reconciliation.

Jesus suffered violent evil that far surpassed what happened to Joseph. His life was not spared; His "wicked brothers" had their way with Him. Yet while the Jewish Council meant evil, God intended it as good. Using the Sanhedrin as He had Joseph's brothers, God moved His chosen Deliverer to the time and place of salvation. For Joseph, it was Pharaoh's courts; for Jesus, it was Calvary's cross.

Just as the crime against Christ was greater, so is the reconciliation. Joseph forgave his brothers' sins against him. Jesus forgives all sins against God and man. We need not fear divine wrath: Jesus bore it in His Passion that we might know God's grace.

**Dear Jesus, as You suffered evil for our good, grant
that we trust that Your good overcomes evil in our lives. Amen.**

MONDAY, LENT 2 — READ JOB 21:1–9 / PSALM 55:16–23

Deceiving Disappearance

Natural disasters, transportation accidents, wars, terrorist attacks, personal tragedies, and family crises—how can a loving God allow these to happen to anyone? Why do they befall "innocent victims"? Especially, why do Christians suffer them?

When we're caught in the middle of calamity, we often find ourselves wondering, "Where is God? Why did this happen? Why isn't He helping?" It pains us even more when unbelievers and blatant sinners sometimes seem to avoid such disasters or profit from them. Job certainly wrestled with the wicked prospering while his life was falling apart.

God sometimes shows why and how He works through such events: Joseph's restoration in Genesis 50, the Tower of Siloam in Luke 13, and the man born blind in John 9 come to mind. At other times, He leaves us wondering. Job never got a plain answer.

Yet even when God hides His purpose, He reveals His presence. Our Suffering Servant participated in our pain. He invites us to cast our burden on Him. While we live in this world, we may continue facing the horrible consequences of Adam's fall. When evil strikes, Christ assures us that He is already with us.

While evidence of evil lies plainly before all, the Christian knows that Christ took this evil upon Himself that He might grant final release. He does this not by righting all wrongs in this life nor by giving "peaceful" oblivion in death. Instead, He grants strength to endure, courage to conquer, and faith that in Him we will be granted eternal peace.

Lord Jesus, bounteous giver Of light and life divine,
You did my soul deliver; To You I all resign.
You have in mercy bought me With blood and bitter pain;
Let me, since you have sought me, Eternal life obtain. Amen.
(*LW* 257:2 [*LSB* 689])

TUESDAY, LENT 2

READ ROMANS 8:28–39
PSALM 9:7–14

Hidden Might, Revealed Mercy

"*We know,*" Paul tells us. We know that Jesus suffered and died for us . . . that we are saved by grace through faith in Christ . . . that we will live forever in heaven . . . that "for those who love God all things work together for good" and that nothing "will be able to separate us from the love of God in Christ Jesus our Lord" (Romans 9:28, 39).

So why do we feel so helpless? Why do these words sound so cliché when we stand with funeral mourners? Why doesn't God reach out and fix things now? How can Paul ask with such irritating calmness, "If God is for us, who can be against us?"

The apostle realized that, as much as he desired to depart and be with Christ, God's purpose was to keep him in this world as witness to the Savior. Paul celebrated opportunities to suffer for the Lord because he knew that it was good for himself and a blessing to others.

As God strengthened Paul's faith and commitment through trial, He also made Paul a testimony to His presence. Likewise, our tragedies and sorrows become tools for God to strip away reliance on the things of this life while also showing that we endure them because Christ who endured Calvary lives in us.

God doesn't want mindless parroting of these words of faith. He tests us that we might know His mercy. Christ veiled His might to suffer for us: He resisted Satan's wilderness temptation; He resisted coming down from the cross. He invites us to meekly take up our cross and follow Him, that an unbelieving world would say, "See what faith these Christians have!" and seeing, believe in Him and live.

> God, grant us in Christ to accept Your will, to know
> Your mercy, and to offer ourselves as living sacrifices
> to the glory of His name. Amen.

WEDNESDAY, LENT 2

READ ISAIAH 53:4–5
PSALM 103:1–5

The Wounded Healer

When justice catches up with the criminal, normal reaction to his punishment is, "He got what he deserved." It seems that way for the Suffering Servant as we read Isaiah 53:4. However, the next verse points out that He got what *we* deserved—and now gives us what we need.

Our Great Physician operates differently than does our family doctor. Our doctors give us advice, pills, and shots. They attempt to chase away our afflictions by applying years of education and experience to our condition. Jesus, on the other hand, doesn't just dispense diagnoses and drugs. He actually took our disease, our pain, our physical, emotional, mental, and spiritual afflictions upon Himself. To undo the damage sin's effect has on our systems, He allowed sin's consequences to inflict Him.

Cartoons often show a fat, chain-smoking doctor telling his patient, "You've gotta quit the cigarettes and go on a diet." The humor comes from an underlying truth: The doctor is often in worse shape than the patient; the physician himself needs healing.

In ordinary life, the doctor becomes the patient either because of self-inflicted problems (overeating, smoking, and the like) or because he is powerless against accident or illness. Not so, Jesus: He could have fully and completely resisted illness and injury but allowed them to happen that He might bear the full curse of the fall.

How does Jesus know your every weakness? By personal experience. How do you know the cure? By knowing Jesus. He who took our afflictions upon Himself invites you to take every concern to Him.

What a friend we have in Jesus, All our sins and griefs to bear!
What a privilege to carry Everything to God in prayer!
Oh, what peace we often forfeit; Oh, what needless pain we bear—
All because we do not carry Ev'rything to God in prayer!
(LW 516:1 [LSB 770])

Daily Devotions

THURSDAY, LENT 2

READ MARK 10:46–52
PSALM 146

The Blind See

One of the most common ailments of biblical times was blindness. It remains a serious problem in much of the world today for many of the same reasons. Some eye diseases are often extremely contagious and some congenital and hereditary ailments may escape early diagnosis.

Bartimaeus was one of many people who received the gift of sight from our Lord. Although unable to see with his eyes, his spiritual vision seems to have been 20/20. Moved by the Spirit, the blind beggar called out to the Son of David for mercy. Jesus heard and gladly answered the prayer.

We note that Christ banished blindness: Did He also bear it? In a way, He did. While Scripture doesn't clearly tell what happened to the Suffering Servant's vision during the dark night of His arrest and trial or the gloomy day of His death, we can well imagine that His own sight was severely impaired at times. We know how the guard blindfolded Him during their taunting and can imagine that the sweat and blood pouring down often clouded His vision. It is possible He could barely see either His tormentors or His mother and beloved disciple at the foot of the cross.

Yet He clearly saw our need for redemption and blindly persisted until the bitter end. He personally experienced the dark of sightlessness even as He procured the cure for our spiritual blindness.

He comes, from thickest films of vice
To clear the mental ray
And on the eyeballs of the blind
To pour celestial day. (TLH 66:3 [LSB 349])

**Thank You, Lord, for bearing our blindness
that we might see You clearly. Amen.**

FRIDAY, LENT 2

READ LUKE 5:17–26
PSALM 147:1–6

Free from Paralysis

A few people reading or having these devotions read to them suffer from permanent paralysis of one kind or another. Whether by accident or illness, the loss of motion severely restricts our movement. Even if only temporary, because of cast, splint, or other immobilization, no one desires being unable to feed oneself, to scratch an itch, or to return embraces.

When this befalls us, do we have a Savior who carried this affliction? Did the Suffering Servant know the terrible restriction of paralysis?

At the height of His Passion, Jesus knew exactly how it feels to be held immobile. On the cross, He couldn't bend or stretch. He couldn't rub tender spots, wipe His eyes, scratch His itches, or fend off the insects that doubtless came to feed on His blood and sweat.

He voluntarily entered physical paralysis in order to free us from sin's immobilizing hold on our lives. He allowed Himself to be bound and stretched out so that we might escape the inability to act according to God's will. The signs of healing He worked during His ministry pointed to the greater healing He effected on the cross.

By willing Himself immobile, He earned forgiveness for us when doubt or selfishness paralyze us and prevent good works. He also claimed solidarity with those whose physical lives remain wrapped in paralysis. The easy freedom with which He moved and appeared among the disciples following His resurrection bears promise for similar freedom for all believers when we are raised from the dead. Even as our spirits are free now, we will also be physically free in the resurrection.

Dear Lord, release us from sin's paralysis that we might freely serve our Father who sent You. Make us especially mindful of our physically challenged brothers and sisters that we might tend to their needs in response to Your love for us. Amen.

Daily Devotions

SATURDAY, LENT 2

READ LUKE 1:68–79
PSALM 89:46–52

The Lord Remembers

Alzheimer's—one of the scariest words in any language. Its victims begin forgetting little things, then important engagements, close friends, their children, their spouses, and even themselves. Sometimes symptoms advance quickly, but often it moves slowly enough that its sufferers realize what is happening.

Christians facing Alzheimer's in themselves or loved ones frequently worry about even forgetting God. After all, He tells us, "*Remember* also your Creator in the days of your youth, before the evil days come" (Ecclesiastes 12:1). More specifically, He says, "*Remember* Jesus Christ, risen from the dead" (2 Timothy 2:8). God invites and commands us to know, believe, and remember Him who suffered and died for us.

This dreadful disease can neither remove the blessings bestowed by Christ nor tear us from our loving God. At John the Baptizer's naming, Zechariah rejoiced that Israel's God would "show the mercy promised to our fathers and to *remember* his holy covenant" (Luke 1:72). Evidently, God really wanted to emphasize the point because Zechariah's name means "the Lord has remembered."

In carrying our afflictions, the Suffering Servant takes away the curse of forgetting the Lord, not only through accident or illness but especially through sinful neglect. In the resurrection, God will heal physical amnesia and restore full mental faculties.

While we still struggle in this life, we have confidence that even if we cannot remember Him, God will never forget us. We may not remember the "little things"; we may almost completely forget everything. The Lord, however, remembers each of us dear "little things," His precious children. In His grace, He "blots out [our] transgressions" and "will not remember [our] sins" (Isaiah 43:25).

> *Assist my soul, too apt to stray,*
> *A stricter watch to keep;*
> *If ever I forget your way,*
> *Restore your wand'ring sheep. Amen.* (LW 392:3 [LSB 707])

Our Suffering Savior

Lent

Week Three

THIRD SUNDAY IN LENT

READ JOHN 11:17–44
PSALM 61

He Hears, We Listen

By the time He came to Bethany, Jesus had already healed numbers of people. Blindness, deafness, crippling afflictions, mental illnesses, and demonic possessions all met their match in Him. Now He faced "the last enemy . . . death" (1 Corinthians 15:26).

Perhaps remembering how Martha had busied herself with earthly preparations as He taught eternal lessons (Luke 10:38–41), Jesus made sure that she truly had been listening. Then He ventured to the tomb. After giving thanks that His Father heard Him, He spoke to the last person we'd expect to listen to Him: "Lazarus, come out."

The disciples earlier marveled that a storm listened (Luke 8:25); now, all present discovered that even a corpse could hear. Death's deafness couldn't defeat the One who hears our prayers. But while a dead man heard, many of the living didn't. While some saw and "believed in *Him*," others only believed that the event happened and planned to make sure it would never happen again.

The Servant knew this sign of salvation would seal His death warrant. Those who refused to listen to Him would hear only each others' plots against His life. Meanwhile, those whose spiritual ears were quickened believed and confessed that He was "the Christ, the Son of God."

Jesus turned a deaf ear to Satan's early temptations in the wilderness. He refused to listen to calls to abandon His mission, even when His own disciples voiced them. He ignored the taunts and jeers voiced toward His cross. Instead, He heard our cries for rescue and brought healing for our spiritual deafness by listening only to His Father's call. Through Word and Spirit, He creates people who hear His Word and believe that He is "the Resurrection and the Life."

Lord Jesus, forgive our deafness to Your Word and grant that we might listen to You and live in Your kingdom. Amen.

MONDAY, LENT 3

READ ACTS 3:1–10
PSALM 18:28–36

Limping, Walking, and Running

A popular hymn begins, "Let us ever walk with Jesus, follow His example pure." While that is exactly what God wants us to do, our fallen nature renders it impossible. Sin's crippling effect is stronger and more complete than any physical handicap we might suffer.

During His ministry, Jesus walked up and down Judea, Galilee, and Samaria. We can visualize Him sometimes bouncing joyfully down a road with a spring in His step while other times trudging up a steep and rocky trail, deeply wearied yet facing miles more to travel. Especially vivid in our minds is His dragging the cross from Jerusalem to Golgotha, staggering under the load.

By assuming the crushing weight of our sins along with the wood of the cross, the Suffering Servant intimately acquainted Himself with the crippling burdens humanity bears in body and soul. Drawing upon every bit of His fast-fading strength, He willed Himself to the finish line (John 19:30) of His life's race.

Our inability to walk the Father's path finds forgiveness in Him who never departed the way. The lame who were healed by Him and His disciples testify to the ultimate healing won at Calvary, given in Baptism, and completed in the resurrection.

Our sins remitted, we aren't just limping down the trail to the New Jerusalem. By His grace, we "lay aside every weight, and sin which clings so closely," and "run with endurance the race that is set before us" (Hebrews 12:1). Unable by our own power to lift a finger to do good works, Christ calls us into actively "walking and leaping and praising God," body and soul, heart and mind.

Only Jesus can impart Balm to heal the wounded heart,
Peace that flows from sin forgiv'n, Joy that lifts the soul to heav'n,
Faith and hope to walk with God In the way that Enoch trod.
(LW 285:3 [LSB 611])

Lord Jesus, grant us "faith and hope to walk with God in the way that Enoch trod." Amen.

Daily Devotions

TUESDAY, LENT 3

READ JOHN 19:31–36
PSALM 51:7–12

Cutting to the Heart

Chest pains, shortness of breath. Pulse races, then slows to a crawl. Pale, sweating. Something terrible is happening and you—who never liked doctors—call the emergency number. You hear, "Call an ambulance, and get to the emergency room immediately!" Upon arrival, you find out that you're having a heart attack.

The ER surgeon springs into action. You're scrubbed clean of dirt and germs, laid bare on a table, and attached to a monitor. Oh, no! This is worse than you thought. Your heart is totally worthless: Cardiac disease so bad that it damaged every other part of your body.

Emergency transplant offers the cure, but who can donate? Others similarly diseased surround you. Yet keeping your own heart will destroy you. "You must trust me," the surgeon says. "What I'm going to do will bring unimaginable hurt first. But I will heal you." How you consented, you cannot understand. Nothing can mask the pain as his knife cleaves your breast. He reaches in, carves out the diseased organ before it can muster another damaging beat, and casts it away.

Eyes filled with tears, he hands the blade to another. "Do it quickly," he says. The attendant cuts out your surgeon's heart, places it in your empty breast, and stitches it into place as the surgeon lies dead on the floor. Immediately, warmth and life flow throughout your body.

Your Suffering Servant entered a world so broken and came to a people so diseased that nothing short of direct donation from Him could ever bring healing. He placed Himself into the violent hands of others, allowing Himself to be wounded unto death that you might have His life. He created your new heart by giving you His own.

Your Son came to suffer for me, Gave himself to rescue me,
Died to heal me and restore me, Reconciled and set me free.
Jesus' cross alone can vanquish These dark fears and soothe
   this anguish. Amen. (**LW 233:3** [**LSB 608**])

WEDNESDAY, LENT 3

READ ISAIAH 53:6
PSALM 95

Straying Sheep

While the primary application of the word *stray* belongs to the animals of flock and herd, a study of Scripture shows how often God applies it to humankind. He applies it to the individual, as in straying from the marriage bed. He accuses a nation, Israel, of straying from His Word. He warns His Church not to stray from the truth. Each warning and every accusation stem from the sad truth that "all we like sheep have gone astray."

This straying began in Eden. Adam set his own course away from the clear and simple command to not eat from the one tree. His fall dragged down his entire posterity: "All we" are born outside the safety of the sheepfold. "All we" willfully follow our desires and exercise our own wills. "All we" are targets for earthly predators and, even worse, for Satan's savage assaults.

The consequences of straying include discontent, disease, disaster, and death. No evil common to man would have any power over us if each was not what we confess in corporate worship, "a lost and condemned sinner."

Whether we stray willfully or through weakness, the same end awaits us. There is only one safe haven, and it is with our Lord Jesus. As the "Lamb of God," He never strayed from the path His Father set before Him: Thus, He was the perfect sacrifice, earning forgiveness for our straying. As the "Good Shepherd," He continues to lead us on a righteous path through this life and to the safe pasture of heaven.

When their sheep have lost their way, Faithful shepherds
  go to seek them;
Jesus watches all who stray, Faithfully to find and take them
In his arms that they may live—Jesus sinners will receive.
(LW 229:3 [LSB 609])

**Lord Jesus, lead, guide, and protect me.
Find and restore me when I lose my way. Amen.**

Daily Devotions

THURSDAY, LENT 3

READ ISAIAH 50:4–11
PSALM 119:9–16

A Firmly Set Face

Today's reading is the third of the four Servant Songs in Isaiah. It introduces the suffering that the final Song details. This prophecy notes how steadfast the Suffering Servant would be: "I have set my face like a flint, and I know that I shall not be put to shame." Flint is a tough, hard rock. This Servant knows it will take absolute resolve to continue along the path the Lord set before Him. He says, "Bring it on!"

Luke 9:51 shows that Jesus was, indeed, the One who came to fulfill the office of Suffering Servant: "When the days drew near for him to be taken up, he set his face to go to Jerusalem." He knew that one day soon He'd go up Mount Zion, enter Jerusalem, and face arrest, horrible torture, and shameful death.

Contrast His focused dedication with our often feeble and halfhearted devotion to our place in the kingdom. We may make rock-solid declarations of intent, as did Peter. Without His help, these noble desires crumble. Without His forgiveness, they would be held against us as examples of our easily distracted and constantly straying natures.

Jesus spoke of turning the other cheek (Luke 6:29) already anticipating the blows His own cheeks would receive. He wouldn't depart from the path but would climb "to Jerusalem" and certain death. Yet as hard as He set His face, He never hardened His heart. Instead, He fed, healed, and forgave. As steadfastly as He faced His doom, He now sends His Spirit to guide you to steadfastly face your deliverance, "looking to Jesus . . . who for the joy that was set before him endured the cross" (Hebrews 12:2).

Lord, keep us steadfast in Your Word;
Curb those who by deceit or sword
Would wrest the kingdom from Your Son
And bring to naught all He has done. (*LW* 334:1 [*LSB* 655])

FRIDAY, LENT 3

READ EZEKIEL 34:1–10
PSALM 49:13–15

Sinful Shepherds

Christians know that Jesus is our Good Shepherd. Sometimes we forget that He calls others to work with Him as shepherds. In Ezekiel's times, these were prophets and priests. Today we have Christian pastors and teachers. Our word *pastor* comes from the Latin for "shepherd" and faithful pastors know they are to shepherd Christ's sheep.

False prophets haven't disappeared. Some still enter the ministry unprepared; others come quite ready—ready to take advantage of the flock. False teachings continue. "Innovative" preachers and theologians subtly twist Scripture, slowly leading their listeners to follow lies.

Should we disregard those who preach and teach in our churches? Should you worry that your pastor is leading his flock to perdition? Probably not. However, the lambs should know their Good Shepherd's voice, His message of forgiveness clearly recorded in the Scriptures. They must compare what Christ says with what their shepherds say.

Sometimes the words of false shepherds sound sweeter and more enticing than the words of the Good Shepherd. Sheep may rebel when they hear of straight paths, narrow gates, and burdensome crosses. But if pastors don't clearly teach and proclaim these things as part of the full counsel of God, they are not true under-shepherds of the Good Shepherd and they don't have our eternal welfare at heart. And while the Lord holds accountable these false teachers, He doesn't excuse those who follow them instead of Him.

Thus, we ask both for faithful pastors who preach the Word with power and for discernment to take the Scriptures to heart that we might judge the doctrine we hear preached and follow the right Voice, even if it leads us, for a time, over a difficult trail.

God of the prophets, bless the prophets' sons;
Elijah's mantle on Elisha cast.
Each age its solemn task may claim but once;
Make each one nobler, stronger than the last.
(LW 258:1 [LSB 682])

SATURDAY, LENT 3

READ EZEKIEL 34:17–24
PSALM 119:33–40

Selfish Sheep

While we usually think of "lost sheep" as those completely removed from contact with the Christian Church, the Lord cautions those who are closer to home. The picture He paints in today's reading points toward those within the Church. It's not any stretch to think that Paul may have had this passage in mind when he rebuked Corinth for its selfish mockery of the Lord's Supper (1 Corinthians 11:17–22).

Do we sometimes have a false sense of our own importance? Even as we confess our sins, might we also be peeking to see if the "real" sinners are also confessing? Do we seek positions of authority in the congregation mainly because we think our ideas are better than those of others? Obviously these problems regularly plague the Church and individuals within her—otherwise, why are books purporting to fix misguided Christians and dysfunctional congregations so popular?

Sadly, we see that merely gathering in a Christian congregation is no guarantee that we believe or act as Christ's people. We cannot make ourselves unselfish. Without a caring shepherd, the sheep stray. Without a wise king, each does what is right in his own eyes without regard for others.

To act as one holy people, we must gather about one Shepherd, one King. In Ezekiel 34, the Lord calls Him His "servant David." The Suffering Servant fulfilled and completed the office held by David. The shepherd boy who became king, the man who ruled and healed the nation of Israel after Saul tore it apart—he foreshadowed our great Shepherd King. In infinite majesty, He rules from heaven; in intimate love He calls, guides, feeds, and strengthens us through Word and Sacraments.

Lord Jesus, think on me
And purge away my sin;
From selfish passions set me free
And make me pure within. Amen. (LW 231:1 [LSB 610])

Our Suffering Savior

Lent

Week Four

FOURTH SUNDAY IN LENT

READ DEUTERONOMY 6:1–8
PSALM 25:1–10

Misleading Leaders

The bellwether was an important part of many flocks. This mature, steady sheep knew where to go, wouldn't stampede, and responded to the shepherd's commands. A bell hung from its neck and the rest of the flock learned to go where it heard the ringing. Similarly, many herds of cattle were led by a "bell cow."

Among young people, parents are the prime bellwethers. Children don't have to be taught to follow parental examples; they pick things up by observation. To the chagrin of parents, this means they often learn our bad habits and words better than the good.

Later on, teachers, schoolmates, coaches, scout leaders, and others become our bellwethers. Each provides some sort of guidance, yet all are responsible to their own leaders and guiding principles. There are many styles of coaching. But a soccer coach who instructs his team to throw the ball into the net isn't leading according to the game's rules. Or he may know and correctly teach all the rules but never work on his team's conditioning.

Sound ridiculous? Many of our bellwethers throughout life don't clearly know where they're going and they mislead all who follow. That's why, when others depend upon our spiritual guidance, we must know clearly the Way to heaven.

If we follow Jesus as we imagine Him rather than Jesus as He is, we mislead not only ourselves but also families, classes, or entire congregations who follow us. As our Good Shepherd leads by grace with a full knowledge of His Father's will, so each of us in positions of authority succeed only by grace as we hear and follow our Shepherd's voice. As we lead, we must lead to the Lord; as we follow, we must follow leaders who hear His voice.

**Grant, dear Father, that we follow where Jesus leads
and lead others, especially our own families, where He is. Amen.**

MONDAY, LENT 4

READ LUKE 15:1–7
PSALM 119:169–176

Little Lost Lambs

Who's more terrified when parent and child separate in a crowded store? Children may panic because they've lost the person who keeps them feeling secure, imagining all sorts of scary scenarios. Parents almost certainly fear because they watch, hear, and read the news—they know how much evil can happen to lost children. If either of these has ever happened to you, what joy came from your reunion!

Believers usually don't leave the Shepherd's protective presence all at once. Distracted or bored, we slowly drift apart. Like children, we often don't give any thought to our circumstances. We're too busy paying attention to the bright temptations surrounding us to realize that we've put ourselves in grave danger.

Our Savior knows what predators lurk, waiting for us to step outside His protection. Satan licks his chops as a fresh kill draws closer, blissfully unaware of its fate. It is no small wonder that the Shepherd springs immediately into action. The Word already heard and kept in the back of our minds comes clearly to the forefront as we realize how far away we've moved from Christ. His call sounds clearly as we recollect Scriptures, hymns, and, perhaps, even sermons that focus on the safety of His presence.

As the shepherd in the parable physically went and retrieved the lost sheep, so our Good Shepherd physically rescued each of us. The parabolic shepherd, however, endured nothing like the tale's Teller. While we may picture the former climbing hills or crawling through thick brush to rescue his missing charge, we know that Christ crawled out of Jerusalem under the cross, climbing the hill of His own death. What joy He had in claiming each of us as His! What celebration as He reclaims us when we stray!

Lord Jesus, whenever I find myself lost, remind me that You have already found me and will bring me safely home. Amen.

TUESDAY, LENT 4

READ JOHN 10:1–18
PSALM 23

The Good Shepherd

The pictures of shepherd and sheep throughout Scripture all point to Christ and His Church. No other safety or salvation exists apart from faith and outside His flock. A fallen world, fed Satan's lies, pouts about this exclusivity. Lost sinners don't realize that they are either sinful or lost. They treat the lies they believe as "gospel truth" without ever knowing the truth of the Gospel.

There is only one Way, one Door, one Truth, one Life, one Good Shepherd. So while Satan drums up discontent over exclusion, the Church answers with a message of joyful inclusion: The Servant suffered not to save good people, but wicked, perverse people. The Church remains the only true flock but the Shepherd welcomes all into His midst.

"I have other sheep," says Jesus. For them, as for the lost sheep of Israel, He laid down His life. The only exclusion is for those who refuse rescue, who won't hear or heed their Rescuer's voice.

He emptied the cup of His life that ours might be filled. He traversed death's valley that it might not be the gate to hell but the entrance to eternal bliss. He endured bitterness to give His dear lambs bliss. His devotion to the flock brought Him death that He might bring us life.

His sheep know His voice. It calls us to repentance and new life. It calls us to spread the Good News and to live in its light. On the Last Day, it will call the living and the dead to final judgment and will call the believers home. The sheep listen to their Shepherd now that they might know His voice through all eternity.

Oh, ever be our guide, Our shepherd, and our pride,
  Our staff and song.
Jesus, O Christ of God,.By your enduring Word
Lead us where you have trod; Make our faith strong.
(LW 471:4 [LSB 864])

Our Suffering Savior

WEDNESDAY, LENT 4

READ ISAIAH 53:7
PSALM 39

Silent Suffering

Literature and history abound with illustrations of the silence of death and grave. Yet the death of the Suffering Servant is also news to be shouted out. Another Passion hymn bids, "Sing, my tongue, the glorious battle!" (*LW* 117)

The exquisite silence of the dying Savior gives eloquent voice to His Church's song. The One who deserved no evil suffered the evil we deserved. We who often complain bitterly over deserved consequences are forgiven by One who refused to complain as He bore the ultimate consequence of our sin. Our noblest hymns only weakly approximate the power of divine love at work in Christ's Passion.

Before any other response, pondering the Servant's suffering leads us also to silent awe: This is what God meant when He threatened death and hell for sinners. This is the wages of sin paid to the One who didn't earn them. This is our pain and horror, our abandonment and damnation we see before us on the cross. Small wonder that this same Servant Song declares "kings shall shut their mouths because of him" (52:15).

As we realize that the horrors He endured won our salvation, we move from silence before His pain to praising His "glorious battle." For the benefit of others, we cannot remain silent. Unbelievers need to hear in order to believe. Fellow believers need to hear that they might be strengthened in the Faith and comforted in their own times of need.

Silently we receive Christ into our lives; aloud we confess His presence to others. Silently we hear; aloud we respond.

Help me speak what's right and good And keep silence on occasion;
Help me pray, Lord, as I should, Help me bear my tribulation;
Help me die and let my spirit Everlasting life inherit. (*TLH* 411:7)

Daily Devotions

THURSDAY, LENT 4

READ PROVERBS 17:27–28
PSALM 34:11–18

A Fool and His Mouth

"A fool and his money are soon parted" while a fool and his mouth is a life-long partnership. Echoing Scripture, secular proverbs testify to the error of foolish speech: "Open mouth, insert foot" summarizes the problem. President Lincoln, Samuel Johnson, and Mark Twain are but a few who've said something like "Better to keep your mouth shut and be thought a fool than to open it and remove all doubt."

The crucifixion wasn't the only time when Jesus refused to open His mouth to engage in what would have been foolish, futile discourse. When men closed their hearts to Him, He often closed His mouth to them. He knew that we cannot argue people into faith. Sometimes scoffers must suffer our silence that they might hear their own foolishness accuse them.

We're often uncomfortable with silence or worried that we must say something—anything—in response to another's unbelief. These are normally the worst times to start talking because we then usually "remove all doubt" about our own knowledge and wisdom.

The gift of silence allows us to listen to our Lord's voice. It gives us opportunity to think and to reflect upon His Word. Rather than blurting the first words that come to our tongues, keeping quiet lets us find and assemble the right words that come from mind and heart.

God doesn't impose a gag order on His people. He does, however, demand accountability for what we say. Thus, we do well to respond only when a response will be fruitful while restraining our tongues when they'll only stir up strife or cast shame upon our Savior. And when we do foolishly speak, we pray that our ever-wise Redeemer would forgive us and teach us wise words and prudent silence.

Lord, rescue us from the folly of our own words and grant us instead the wisdom of Your Word. Amen.

FRIDAY, LENT 4

READ EXODUS 20:7
PSALM 116

Sanctified Silence

A communion hymn exhorts, "Let all mortal flesh keep silence" (*LW* 241:1). Often, this is our best response to the Second Commandment. On Sinai, God said, "You shall not take the name of the Lord your God in vain" (Exodus 20:7).

In the Small Catechism, Martin Luther explained, "We should fear and love God so that we do not curse, swear, use satanic arts, lie, or deceive by His name, but call upon it in every trouble, pray, praise, and give thanks" (p. 9–10). Silently receiving His Word is part of honoring His name. Wrongly invoking or falsely swearing by it are evil. So is seeking aid in the name of anyone or anything other than the true God.

Along with sanctified silence come blessed opportunities to cry out to God, to "pray, praise, and give thanks." In silence and speech, the Servant kept this commandment perfectly. He worshiped in temple and synagogue, read and taught the Word, and prayed faithfully. He accepted His Father's will without complaint.

Sadly, our fallen natures descend from those who "exchanged the truth about God for a lie and worshiped and served the creature rather than the Creator" (Romans 1:25). Unconverted, we would follow Adam, listening to Satan's lies while not speaking His truth to those who need to hear it while trusting in all else but God.

Christ's keeping of this commandment is credited to us. His silent acceptance of the Father's will and His life of prayer and proclamation count as our righteousness. Though we remain silent when God would have us speak, call wrongly on His name, or place our trust in another, Jesus paid the price for our transgression. And as the living Christ dwells within us, He leads us back to God-pleasing lives of sanctified silence and blessed voice.

In silence and in speech, dear Jesus, lead us to ever hallow the name of the Lord our God. Amen.

Daily Devotions

SATURDAY, LENT 4 — READ JAMES 3:1–12 / PSALM 102:1–8

Wagging Tongues

Would we ever dare to say about God some of the things we speak concerning each other? James reminds us, "With [the tongue] we bless our Lord and Father, and with it we curse people who are made in the likeness of God" (3:9). We can go through an entire Sunday service singing, praying, and praising, then start speaking ill of our neighbor before we even reach our cars. "From the same mouth come blessing and cursing. My brothers, these things ought not to be so" (3:10).

The Holy Spirit inspired James to make this close comparison between the Second and the Eighth Commandments. Of course, there are differences. With God, no truth we can tell about Him could ever damage His reputation, for God is always truthful. With man, we ought never lie and harm another's good name and we must also be careful with the truth, speaking it only when it edifies. The Small Catechism reminds us that keeping the Eighth Commandment is more than not lying about others. It encourages us to "defend [our neighbor], speak well of him, and explain everything in the kindest way" (p. 11).

Often, the worst gossip is the truth. And not one of us, even the most pious saint, possesses a life so pure that it is without sin. God urges us to be active and zealous in building up each other. He bids us speak to others the same blessings that we receive through His Son, using our mouths to forgive, honor, praise, and encourage.

A lying witness never be, Nor foul your tongue with calumny.
The cause of innocence embrace, The fallen shield from disgrace.
Have mercy, Lord! (LW 331:9)

Lord Jesus, as the words of this hymn describe Your speech before others, so grant us to speak or remain silent to our neighbor's greatest benefit. Amen.

Lent

Week Five

FIFTH SUNDAY IN LENT

READ ISAIAH 42:1–9
PSALM 34:1–10

Serving Self

This introductory Servant Song anticipates the later silence of the Lord's Anointed. Quiet, humble service looks totally out of place in a self-serving world. As so many around Him shouted, "Look at me!" the Savior said, "Look to My Father."

How many truly humble, serving people can you name? How many proud, self-aggrandizing people? People who are already famous, even if for inconsequential reasons, hire publicists to make themselves look even more important. Multi-million dollar athletes and recording stars surround themselves with fawning entourages in order to continually feed their already bloated selves additional empty praises.

We only have a few instances recorded of Jesus using advance messengers. When He did so, it was promotion of His message of repentance and salvation, not of Him. When He did take special pains to prepare people for His later arrival, He sent His disciples into Jerusalem before He entered on Palm Sunday. This, however, turned out differently than the crowd expected.

Even Jesus' "Triumphal Entry" into Jerusalem wasn't accompanied by boasting speech or self-promotion. With opportunity to stand before the people and proclaim Himself King, our Lord chose instead to continue onward as the Suffering Servant. His discourses, whether public or private, focused on repentance, judgment, and His impending Passion.

Having passed through His Passion and into glory, Jesus still points to the Father, mediates with the Father, and places the Father above Himself. By His grace, we need not fret about promoting ourselves in His kingdom, for we know that in Baptism, He has already anointed and declared us as His kings and priests—and there is no higher office to which we might aspire.

Forbid it, Lord, that I should boast
Save in the death of Christ, my God;
All the vain things that charm me most,
I sacrifice them to his blood. Amen. **(LW 114:2 [LSB 425])**

MONDAY, LENT 5

READ LUKE 22:39–46
PSALM 46

A Quiet Place to Pray

Luther wrote that it is good "to let prayer be the first business of the morning and the last at night. Guard yourself carefully against those false, deluding ideas which tell you, 'Wait a little while. I will pray in an hour; first I must attend to this or that.' Such thoughts get you away from prayer into other affairs which so hold your attention and involve you that nothing comes of prayer for that day" (*Luther's Works* 43:193).

As the day described in Luke 22 ended, Jesus slipped off with the disciples to a quiet place for prayer. With arrest, trial, and torture looming, His mind certainly was busy. What a great excuse to delay prayer for a more convenient time!

He knew, though, that quiet hearts come only from His Father. As agony filled Him, Jesus "prayed more earnestly; and his sweat became like great drops of blood falling down to the ground" (22:44). Our Suffering Servant was already engaged in mortal combat with sin, death, and devil. Continuing the festive Passover dinner or losing Himself among the celebrating people of Jerusalem would bring no peace.

We don't carry the weight of the world's sins upon our shoulders, but our own burdens are amply heavy for our weak selves. The quiet resolve Jesus received from His Father is also the Father's gift for all of us who ask.

Jesus knows our trials and temptations. He wrestled with disquiet; now He quiets our hearts. He invites us to give Him our weighty care that He might carry our petitions to His loving Father.

Grant, Lord Jesus, that my healing In Your holy wounds I find.
Cleanse my spirit, will, and feeling; Heal my body, soul, and mind.
When some evil thought within Tempts my wayward heart to sin,
Work in me for its eviction, Weighted by Your crucifixion.
(LW 95:1)

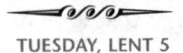

TUESDAY, LENT 5

READ REVELATION 5:6–14
PSALM 144

A New Song

"How silently, how silently this wondrous Gift is given!" These words from "O Little Town of Bethlehem" echo this past week's readings. Lent brings the Nativity to mind. Both center on the Word made flesh. Angelic fanfare announced the incarnation, yet God still slipped His Son so quietly into human history that few noticed.

We might liken the Salvation Story to a grand choral piece introduced by a quiet solo theme. Choir responses base themselves on one central melody, harmonizing with it. The composer-soloist weaves His way through the work, inviting others to join His song—a song that is soft and meditative here, full of vigor and zeal there. No matter the number of singers, one Voice stands out, holding the many together, binding them by what He sings and by how He expresses Himself.

Concluding the earthly song, the Soloist will bring all other voices to a hush: Those singing with Him will kneel in awe; those who've been making noisy perversions of His composition will drop in dread. He'll bid those who've followed His lead and believed in His work to come join the eternal song while those who've resisted are sent to unending, loathsome noise. The song of the Suffering Servant will be remade into the eternal new song of the conquering King. Fallen creation's cacophony of competing voices will never interrupt or drown out eternity's choir.

Christ invites us to begin and end each day listening to His voice guiding, directing, and forgiving. Responding, we harmonize with His theme of salvation in all its varied parts. Lamentations over sin and sorrow turn to sweet songs of joy. Sung amidst earth's off-key lost creatures, our "duets" with Christ invite all to know and love His "new song" and to join us in the choir of the redeemed.

Lord Jesus, keep us even in harmony with Your saving Gospel as we sing Your New Song in thought, word, and deed. Amen.

WEDNESDAY, LENT 5

READ ISAIAH 53:8
PSALM 71:1–6

Justifying Injustice

The arrest and trial of Jesus Christ constitute the largest injustice in humankind's ugly history. No one else was ever convicted by such a combination of blatant lies and misunderstood truth. Thomas Kelly's hymn "Stricken, Smitten, and Afflicted" notes with seeming irony: "The deepest stroke that pierced him Was the stroke that justice gave" (*LW* 116:2).

When we look behind the scenes, however, we see that Kelly wasn't being ironic. While man's injustice was the instrument of Christ's doom, it was directed by God's justice. The Lord used the plots of evil people to satisfy His own just wrath at sin and carry out His plan of salvation.

God's justice doesn't compare with human fairness. We often long to "level the playing field"; God levels *everything* that doesn't meet His idea of perfection. What seems unfair and unjust is that the holy Son of God was made the Suffering Servant. The only good apple in a rotten barrel was blamed for the others' worminess.

Scripture consistently declares divine wrath for human iniquity. God's justice demands death for sin. In His mercy, however, God caused His anger at all mankind to fall upon the perfect Man. Using false testimony bought by fearful scoffers, the Father sent His Son to the cross. Unjust means satisfied God's just end.

With justice over sin met, God uses the Servant's suffering and death to justify sinners. All have died in Christ, so God's righteous anger is met. Through our adoption by water and the Word, He sees those who believe in His Son as He sees Jesus—perfect and holy, justly deserving not doom and death but grace and peace. What a loving Savior! Reversing perverse proceedings, Jesus revealed the truth of His Father's love through the lies of His sin-blinded enemies.

> Thank you, Father, for allowing Your Son's unjust fate
> to secure our justification. Amen.

Daily Devotions

THURSDAY, LENT 5
READ HEBREWS 11:8–19
PSALM 127

Descendants of the Childless

The biblical idea of "justice" is more than courtroom law and order. It involves righting wrongs, defending the defenseless, fixing what's broken, and ordering chaos. One of the gravest "injustices" of biblical times was remaining childless. Believers could hope that Messiah would be born to them or their descendants and all but the wealthiest, regardless of faith, needed children to help with their present work and to provide for them when they were aged and infirm.

Childlessness, perceived as a sign of God's disfavor, would serve to justify unjust behavior toward Him. Barrenness was seen as disgrace and would popularly suggest an underlying sin against even the most pious life. Such thinking anticipated many of the "prosperity gospels" of later days, where having good happen is a sign that God loves you, so receiving evil must mean the opposite.

In the midst of all hangs the childless Son of the Father. Yet even as "good as dead" Abraham was "justified" with "descendants as many as the stars of heaven," so, contrary to appearances, Jesus of Nazareth was "justified" with future generations. Paul writes, "God sent forth his Son, born of woman, born under the law, to redeem those who were under the law, so that we might receive adoption as sons" (Galatians 4:4–5).

The injustice of dying without heirs was removed by the Father's grace. All who believe and have been baptized are the recipients of this grace, for we have been numbered among the multitude who, by the salvific work of the Son, have been called children of the heavenly Father.

And what Your Spirit, Lord, has taught me
To seek from You must needs be such a prayer
As you will grant through Him who bought me
And raised me up to be Your child and heir.
In Jesus' name I boldly seek Your face
And take from You, my Father, grace for grace. (LW 446:4)

FRIDAY, LENT 5

READ GALATIANS 4:1–7
PSALM 130

Justice Delayed

William Gladstone once said, "Justice delayed is justice denied." As he viewed himself as a prime spokesman for the weak and disenfranchised, Gladstone wanted to make sure that the poor had timely hearings in English courts. Otherwise, the rich and powerful could out-wait many of their claims and keep them from a fair decision.

Mankind's wait for the fulfillment of divine justice lasted thousands of years. The Crusher of Satan's head (Genesis 3:15) would descend from the woman, but not in her lifetime—nor during many lives to come. Finally, in "the fullness of time"—divine time, not human—"God sent forth His Son."

Justice was not denied. "When the fullness of time had come," Christ was born. The Servant entered history at the moment of God's choosing. Israel still gathered as a nation. Roman occupation provided the instrument of His torture and death. Chosen witnesses were there to be called, then sent out with His message of reconciliation. The Roman Empire and relative peace throughout the region allowed wide and rapid spread of the Gospel.

Christ's suffering and death completed our great redemption. However, there are still other obstacles and oppressions with which we contend. From the depths of our struggles, we cry out to be freed from poverty, mental and physical illness, or other evils. Sometimes release comes quickly. At others, justice seems denied. Our souls wait while nothing seems to happen.

However, just as our Father accomplished the salvation of mankind at His appointed time, so He will right those wrongs that still afflict us. Maybe not where, when, or how we want or expect, but it will happen for those who trust in Christ. He denies no good thing to the believer but He gives good only at the time He knows best.

**Lord Jesus, teach me to watch and wait in hope
for the hour of my deliverance. Amen.**

Daily Devotions

SATURDAY, LENT 5

READ ISAIAH 25:6–9
PSALM 133

Just Desserts

While we often use the term "just desserts" to mean that someone got deserved punishment, we receive as the "dessert of the justified" completely undeserved salvation from sin, death, and devil through Christ's atoning sacrifice. Even during this penitential season of Lent, God refreshes and restores us with this sweet message.

God instituted the Sabbath as rest and refreshment for the weary. Jesus spent His final Sabbath Day before His Passion with His dear friends Mary, Martha, and Lazarus (John 12:1–10). We must assume that He was very much resting up for the bitterness to come.

The next day, He would ascend Zion, the Mountain of the Lord, into Jerusalem as an adoring crowd praised His name. By week's end, He would die on the city's outskirts. Through all this, He fulfilled the promise that "on this mountain" the Lord would set a most refreshing feast.

"On this mountain" Christ instituted the life-giving Supper of His body and blood. "On this mountain" he drank the bitter cup of suffering and death set before Him by His Father. He suffered and died, yet rose to "swallow up on this mountain" death's funeral pall. As evidence, He left behind "on this mountain" His unneeded burial linens.

The resurrection restored unity between God and man. Its fruits include Christian harmony. Indeed, only when we have "the blessing" of "life forevermore" do we have truly "good and pleasant" brotherly unity.

Enjoy in peace your "just desserts." God delights as you find your refreshment in Him and promises perfect rest and restoration in the Day of our Lord Jesus Christ.

Jesus, refuge of the weary, Blest redeemer, whom we love,
Fountain in life's desert dreary, Savior from the world above:
Often have Your eyes, offended, Gazed upon the sinner's fall;
Yet upon the cross extended, You have borne the pain of all. Amen.
(*LW* 90:1 [*LSB* 423])

Our Suffering Savior

Holy Week

PALM SUNDAY

READ JOHN 12:12–19
PSALM 24

Servant's Entrance

At one time, most wealthy people had servants' entrances to their houses. These were reserved for household workers, deliverymen, and the like. Only wealthy and powerful friends received welcome through the main entrance.

Jesus doubly deserved entry through Jerusalem's main gate. As God of God from all eternity, this was His city where He established the household of David as an eternal kingship. According to His flesh, He descended from King David.

Yet even as Jesus entered the city heralded like a conquering King, He gave signs that He was making the main gate His personal Servant's entrance. He rode a donkey, not a warhorse. He accepted acclaim not with a demand to be crowned king but with humble disregard. He would be crowned in Jerusalem, but with thorns, not gold and jewels.

"His disciples did not understand these things at first, but when Jesus was glorified, then they remembered that these things had been written about him and had been done to him." Sinful flesh is blind to the sacrificial humility of the Suffering Servant. We expect our rulers to be as vain and foolish as we are. Only God-given faith allows us eyes to see Him as both Servant and King, riding in glory to an inglorious death:

> *Ride on, ride on in majesty!*
> *In lowly pomp ride on to die.*
> *Bow Your meek head to mortal pain,*
> *Then take, O Christ Your pow'r and reign.* (LW 105:5 [LSB 441])

Jesus remained a faithful Servant until death. Yet the cross was footstool to His heavenly throne, to which He ascended on the fortieth day of His resurrection. His crown of life He bestows on all who remain faithful to Him until death. He makes it a pleasure to meekly serve Him who served us all.

Preserve us as Your faithful servants, O Lord, that we might also reign under You in majesty forevermore. Amen.

MONDAY IN HOLY WEEK

READ JOHN 12:1–11
PSALM 36:5–10

Serving the Servant

As the resurrected Lazarus reclined at the table with Jesus and the disciples, Martha resumed an earlier responsibility and served the guests from their kitchen. Mary likewise assumed a familiar position, at the feet of Jesus. This time, however, she did more than sit and listen to His words.

The Spirit moved her to anoint Jesus' feet with "expensive ointment" and dry them with her hair. Normally, cleaning a guest's feet either fell to the guest or, in richer homes, to the lowest household servant. Mary confessed by her actions that Jesus was the most exalted person to ever enter their house.

She also echoed the prophetic gift of the Magi's myrrh. This burial spice given the young Jesus foreshadowed His now impending entombment—a fact not lost on Him. Her posture of shameful servitude itself was a picture of His own head bowed in death.

The poor Suffering Servant graciously accepted the rich gift. He would soon respond with an infinitely richer gift, His life for the life of the world. So it goes: No matter how we might pay homage to the Christ, He always honors us more. No matter what we give Him, it comes from what He has already given us.

Yet this doesn't preclude our service, our giving, or our honor. He told the greedy Judas, "The poor you always have with you, but you do not always have me." One of His parting gifts is the privilege and pleasure of continuing His servanthood:

Wondrous honor You have given To our humblest charity
In your own mysterious sentence, "You have done it all to me."
Can it be, O gracious Master, That you deign for alms to sue,
Saying by your poor and needy, "Give as I have giv'n to you"?
(LW 402:3 [LSB 851])

Thank you, Lord, for allowing us
to serve a needy world in Your name. Amen.

TUESDAY IN HOLY WEEK

READ JOHN 12:24–43
PSALM 18:1–7, 17–20

Uplifted and Uplifting

Servants serve. No one engages a laborer to sit and watch while the master works. Why would one make beds, sweep floors, or clean bathrooms before the maid arrived? Even if it's not our servant, who presumes to barge past the doorman? Would we rise from table to help the wait staff bring dinner to the table our host prepares for us?

Why, then, do people try to do the work of the Suffering Servant? The task of lifting one sinner out of hellish dominion is impossible for any fallen human. The weight of anyone's sins crushes their bearer into the very pits of hell. Born in sin, steeped in iniquity, from whence comes the strength necessary to effect our own rescue?

We cannot rise up to throw off the dead load sitting upon us—we *are* the dead load. Dead in trespass, loaded with our birth-sin and the succession of iniquitous thoughts, wicked words, and dastardly deeds, we cannot move ourselves to righteousness.

While Jewish council and Roman troops "helped", He always bore the true load upon Himself. The relatively light weight of His mortal flesh carried the full burden of all sins. Only this called Servant of the Lord had the strength of self to accomplish the task.

Upon resurrection, He stretched out His arms even farther. Through the spread of His Word, He reached out to every corner of the world to find lost sinners and bring them to the safety of His loving embrace. We come because He calls. We are free because He broke death's chains and lifted sin's weight. We remain because He continues to draw us close by Word and Sacrament.

Draw us to you; Our hope renew;
Into your kingdom take us.
Let us all there Your glory share;
Your saints and joint heirs make us. Amen.
(*LW* 153:4 [*LSB* 701])

WEDNESDAY IN HOLY WEEK

READ ISAIAH 49:3–7
PSALM 86:1–13 (14–17)

Increase the Load!

We hear it all the time. In business, it's, "Need something done? Give it to a busy man." In football, the prized running back "gets stronger the more he carries the ball." The Lord established His Servant as the embodiment of Israel: Messiah would unmake their errors and perfectly fulfill their calling before God.

However, the Lord saw much more work for His Servant than the redemption of Israel—this task alone was "too light a thing"! Atoning for all of Israel's sins of thought, word, and deed was too easy; the Lord would increase the load: "I will make you as a light for the nations, that my salvation may reach to the end of the earth" (49:6).

While we buckle and collapse under the Law's weight pressing upon our own sins, the Lord expected His Servant to suffer the crushing burden of all humanity's transgressions. At the same time, He was to spread the light of God's love through the entire world.

God needed something done, so He called upon His Son. The eternal Word—the Doer of His Father's bidding from all eternity, the Agent of Creation—He was the already busy One whom the Father selected to conduct the business of salvation for Israel and all nations.

As His physical strength drained during His final bitter hours of life, His true strength drawn from His Father became more apparent. Where fatigue and pain lead us to surrender the task or lash out against others, the Servant stayed the course, forgiving those who condemned and crucified Him.

By His grace, the Father supplies us with the same strength shown by the Servant. As trials wear us down, we may be confident that in Jesus, God's "power is made perfect in weakness" (2 Corinthians 12:9).

With Your Word and Sacrament, O Christ, strengthen and sustain us until our appointed service is complete. Amen.

HOLY (MAUNDY) THURSDAY

READ JOHN 13:12–16
PSALM 100

Divine Service

On the night He was betrayed, Jesus performed two very different, yet intimately related services for His disciples. As they gathered at the table, He washed their feet, and then fed them the banquet of His own body and blood. Taking these events together, we see that the feast He offers as Head of Table and Host is the result of His humble service as He set Himself lower than the lowest sinner.

Even now, as He rules in glory, the dear Christ actively serves His pilgrim Church. The Germans kept this in mind, calling worship with Holy Communion *Gottesdienst* (God's Work). Some English language hymnals preserve this thought with the "Divine Service." These expressions remind us that, as we gather in the Lord's house, we come not to serve Him, but to receive His service.

Christ our Host invites us to eat the flesh and drink the blood of the silent sacrificial Lamb. Christ our Head and Master gives us the benefits and blessings He earned as Suffering Servant. As He descends to Earth in His Supper, He also raises us up into His heavenly presence. Through the Word proclaimed and by the Word eaten and drunk, He forgives our sins, restores our strength, and refreshes our spirits.

How do we render our thanksgiving for His service? By responding to His call to serve Him. We fear, love, and trust in God and love our neighbor in thought, word, and deed. We gladly and willingly serve our Suffering Servant through prayer and praise and by gladly and willingly giving spiritual and physical aid to those in need, just as He meets our needs.

> *I should have died eternally, But here, repentant kneeling,*
> *Newborn I rise to live the love Found in your strength, Your healing.*
> *Lord, in this sacrament impart Your joy and courage to my heart;*
> *Dead yet alive I praise You!* (**LW 246:5** [**LSB 622**])

GOOD FRIDAY

READ JOHN 19:28–30
PSALM 22:22–31

Task Mastered

The cry of abandonment that begins Psalm 22 forms one of the so-called "seven words from the cross." It underscores the depth of Christ's suffering and the enormity of our sins. It's quite possible that Jesus actually prayed the entire Psalm; even if He didn't, no one familiar with the Scriptures could doubt the source of His lament.

The next in the traditional order of the seven words is "It is finished." When we read the final verse of Psalm 22, we get the same message: "He has done it." The cross-forsaken Son of God told His Father and all who hear Him, "I have done what I was called to do."

"It is finished" wasn't a whimper of resignation but triumph's shout. The Suffering Servant accomplished our salvation, declared so before God and man, and prepared to receive His rest. Nothing remains to be done. No extra works by man, no other miracles by God are needed. Jesus could sleep in death knowing that all Scripture was fulfilled.

Not one command or ordinance of God had His Son broken. Christ kept the Law purely and completely. He resisted each temptation by Satan to forsake His appointed tasks. He denied every desire of His own flesh to make the suffering cease. He refused to cut short His servitude to gain worldly relief.

Done is Christ's perfect service. Finished are sin, death, and devil. As the Good News of the Servant's willing sacrifice spreads, "All the ends of the earth shall remember and turn to the Lord." The world's vain search for a clear conscience ends under the stream of blood-bought forgiveness flowing from the cross.

With "It is finished" you have done,
The course your Father set is run, The victory achieving.
So let us do your work on earth, Your promises believing. Amen.
(LW 108:6)

HOLY SATURDAY

READ MATTHEW 27:57–66
PSALM 118:17–29

The Servant's Sabbath Sleep

Death, the wages of the wicked, took the sinless Suffering Servant while righteous and wealthy Joseph of Arimathea claimed His body and set it in a new tomb. The contrast foretold by Isaiah came to pass: "And they made his grave with the wicked and with a rich man in his death, although he had done no violence, and there was no deceit in his mouth" (53:9). One who never sinned suffered and died like a common criminal; yet He who met the felon's fate was entombed in honor.

Christian burial reflects what a difference this makes. Were it not for Christ's loving sacrifice, our tombs would be prisons and gates to hell. However, because He died for us, the funeral service points to a different end. The processional verses leading to grave-side quote today's Psalm: "Open to me the gates of righteousness, that I may enter through them and give thanks to the LORD." Faith's eyes receive answer in the following verse: "This [grave] is the gate of the LORD; the righteous shall enter through it."

The concluding collect connects us to Jesus' death and resurrection—and also His burial. The grave signifies that all sin and deserve the doom of death. However, the tomb of the Christian also testifies that as our Lord rested in honor from His brutal labors over the three days, His saints will peacefully rest until their own resurrection. This hymn likewise encourages us:

> *Then take comfort and rejoice, For his members Christ will cherish.*
> *Fear not, they will hear his voice; Dying, they will never perish;*
> *For the very grave is stirred When the trumpet's blast is heard.*
> **(LW 266:6 [LSB 741])**

O Firstfruits of the Resurrection, I ask that You love me in life, keep me through death, and restore me to life everlasting. Amen.

EASTER DAY

READ ISAIAH 53:10–12
PSALM 16

Successful Servant

The Apostles' Creed simply states the success of the Suffering Servant: "On the third day He rose again from the dead." It echoes God's eternal confidence in His Christ: The Lord delighted in Him (Isaiah 42:1) who was the "beloved Son" of the Father (Matthew 3:17). As proof that His sacrifice for sin was accepted, "God raised Him from the dead" (Acts 13:30).

If we wonder about God's love for sinful man, we can turn to this: "He rose again from the dead." Baptism saves, absolution forgives, communion unites, and our Savior will raise us up to live forever because "He rose again from the dead."

By worldly standards, Jesus failed miserably. He died poor, homeless, and disgraced. Most of His followers abandoned or disavowed Him. How does any of this make Him a lasting success?

Jesus succeeded *because* He "failed." He failed to sin, to sidestep His Father's bidding; to flee suffering and death. His Father predicted and granted His success, then called Him triumphant from the tomb. He came not to succeed in popularity or power but in service and sacrifice—we know He succeeded because "on the third day He rose again from the dead."

His success redeems our failures. He freed us from the failure of Adam's sin and frees us for lives of successful service. His success continues as we trust in Him for forgiveness, life, and salvation. He claims victory with every lost sheep entering His sheepfold, with each saint taken into eternal rest, with lives lived in His love, and with His Gospel preached to the ends of the earth. Because He lives, we live; because He succeeded, we succeed. In life and death, "we are more than conquerors through him who loved us" (Romans 8:37).

**Lord God, regardless of this life's successes or failures,
grant that we remain confident that we are heirs
of Your Servant's successful sacrifice on our behalf. Amen.**

Daily Devotions

Notes
ASH WEDNESDAY and the Days Following

Notes
LENT: Week One

Notes
LENT: Week Two

Notes
LENT: Week Three

Notes
LENT: Week Four

Notes
LENT: Week Five

Notes
HOLY WEEK